THE PIG POETS

THE
PIG POETS

AN ANTHOLOGY OF
PORCINE POESY

Edited and Annotated by
HENRY HOGGE

HarperCollins*Publishers*

HarperCollinsPublishers
77-85 Fulham Palace Road,
Hammersmith, London W6 8JB

Published by HarperCollins*Publishers* 1995
1 3 5 7 9 8 6 4 2

Copyright © Ralph Rochester 1995

The Author asserts the moral right to be identified
as the author of this work

A catalogue record for this book is available from
the British Library

ISBN 0 00 638439 0

Set in Caslon

Printed by
Scotprint Ltd, Musselburgh, Scotland

Dedicated to Count C.W. with
love and gratitude

Time was when innocent and trim we ran
   warm-bristled in the sun on shapely legs.
Beyond the em'rald palms the golden sand
   beckoned us to a feast of turtles' eggs.

An age ago,
Ah comrade mine!
A golden isle,
A happy, happy time!

Time was when striped and carefree we would play
In jungle paths and glades where we could dig
   the spicy roots that grew along the way,
delicious far beyond the dreams of pig.

An age ago,
Ah comrade mine!
A golden isle,
A happy, happy time

                              H.H.

*A*nd chiefly thou, O Spirit, that does prefer
    Before all temples th'upright heart and pure,
Instruct me, for thou know'st; thou from the first
Wast present, and with mighty wings outspread
Dove-like satst brooding on that vast abyss,
And mad'st it pregnant: what in me is dark
Illumine, what is low raise and support;
That to the height of this great argument
I may assert eternal Provender

And justify the ways of pigs to men.

                                H.H.

CONTENTS

FOREWORD

$\mathcal{T}$HIS weary yet still delightful world has waited long for the Pig Poets. To their siren voices none have cared or dared to listen. Mankind has rightly suspected that the experience of the Pig is somewhat limited. Food, sleep, an occasional frolic in the field and a somewhat casual approach to procreation and other forms of physical contact mean that Pigs sing limited and predictable songs. Moreover, the lives of Pigs are not only brutish but short and it is a lot to ask of the Eater of Bacon and Pork Chops that he should hark to the spiritual effusions of the very animal he eats. Nevertheless, the songs are here, now, before the Reading Public, and, if a man turn away from them on the grounds that they, Poets and Poems, are poor crude things, he himself will be the poorer and cruder for it. No one should dismiss the Poetry of the Pig because it soars to less dizzy heights than the Poetry of the Man. A Man should sooner, in a Johnsonian fit, declare himself amazed that Pigs, some Pigs, are Poets at all, and he should think of them as mute inglorious Miltons able to teach him nothing of God but something of what it means to be a Pig. (*The Reader should note that all the Pig Poets collected here have already paid their debt to Nature and to Man – indeed the Reader may unknowingly have dined on the gammon of one of these same porcine friends of whom nothing now remains but the voice.*)

Poems are written – and I ask no thanks for the huge task that I personally have undertaken in bringing this little book before the Public – so that they may be spoken aloud; or, indeed, sung aloud, for many of these Poems lend themselves to sensitive musical accompaniment. Aloud! Aye! The louder the better. But, in order that we may not forget the sole begetters of the works, I beg the Reader to insist with me that the poems, whether sung or recited, whether in private or before a public, shall be prefaced with a Dedicatory Grunt. The Grunt is to be effected by drawing in the breath rather than by exhaling it, the mouth open and the nostrils flared and the air flowing freely through all three orifices. The Dedicatory Grunt should not be overdone.

Enough! Where I have lead, you are invited to follow.

HENRY HOGGE
The Malthouse Field
Lympstone,
September 1994

GEOFFREY PORKER

A SEMINAL PIG POET[1]

The Sowe of Bathe[2]

A good SOWE was ther of bisyde BATHE.
But she had lost her tayl and that was scathe[3]
Lusty she was, with hipes large of caste[4]
And nipples ech more lufsom than the laste.
In al the pigge-folde, sowe ne was noon
That to the trogh bifore hir sholde goon,
And if ther dide, certayn she wolde not yelde,
But bite thir tayls til that the harlots[5] squeled.
But hir own tayl not noon of them colde finde.
She was bos-eyed, as I do have mynde.[6]

She was a worthy moder al hir lyve,
And piglings hadde she three-score and fyve.[7]

1. Porker has fully earned his traditional title of Father of pig poetry.
2. From the Prologue to Porker's *Corkscrue Tayls*.
3. 'That was scathe' = this was a pity. Cf. the modern German: *das war aber schade*.
4. She had big hips. N.B. 'A good sow should have the shoulders of a princess and the bottom of a cook' (Farmer David Black).
5. 'Harlots': pigs of low birth (used of both sexes).
6. As I recall, she had prominent eyes.
7. An excellent total ; let us suppose 7 litters at an average of 9.2857142 pigs reared per litter.

WILLIAM WOBBLEBOTTOM[1]

THE BOAR OF AVON[2]

Madrigal

*T*AKE O take that snout away,
   That so sweatily did kiss,
And those piggy eyes which once
Bade me dream of porcine bliss,
But my maizemeal bring again,
Bring again!
And my wurzels bring again,
Bring again![3]

1. Wobblebottom was *not* the same pig as Sir Francis 'troughing maketh a full pig' Bacon, the Pig Philosopher.
2. Also known as 'The Sweet Swine of Avon'.

3. The lovelorn Pig Poet has apparently been indulging in the unpiglike behaviour of *giving away* good food.

CHRISTOPHER WALLOWE

AN UNFORTUNATE PIG POET [1]

The Passionate Pig Poet to his Sow

> COME live with me and be my mate
> And share my corner by the gate
> – This ditch and all that it supplies
> Of bugs and slugs and fleas and flies.
>
> There thou shalt sit upon thy hams
> And know the joys of she who crams,
> For breakfast I shall bring thee roses,
> Lunch – a thousand fragrant posies. [2]

1. The 'generous, golden, untidy genius' died young, as is so often the fate of bacon pigs. Wallowe, although bred in Kent, was a Tamworth, distinguished by his rust-red hair, hence 'golden', and his extremely long snout.

2. Wallowe was only one of many Pig Poets who, above all things, enjoyed roses and other flowers to eat. Cf. the memorable lines of the delightful Pig Poet Thomas Pudd:

> It was not in the winter our loving
>   lot was cast,
> It was the time of roses, we
>   munched them as we passed.

And I shall scratch thee with my snout
And cherish all thy parts about,
And if thou think'st such pleasures rate,
Come live with me and be my mate.

ROBERT HEDGEPIG

A PASTORAL PIG POET [1]

Counsel to Piglings

S NUFFLE ye truffles[2] while ye can
   Old Time is still a flying,
And somewhere surely hangs the Pan
   That bits of ye will fry in.

That Frying Pan of Heaven the Sun
   Will wink while ye are hissing,
So trot along and have some fun
   While none of ye is missing.[3]

1. Hedgepig, a Long White Lop-
Eared, lived in Devon.
2. Truffle, genus of edible fungi of
the division *Ascomyceteae*, much loved
by pigs, and found just below the soil,
usually beneath a tree or in wooded
places. As the truffle is not normally
associated with the edge of Dartmoor,
where Hedgepig had his living, this
may be considered pigpoetic license.
3. This little pig poem and that of
Sir John Suckling, 'Encouragements
to a Pigling', below, may be said to
encapsulate the whole of pig
(Baconian) philosophy. 'Pigs all must
perish', yes!, but and therefore 'trot
along and have some fun', or, in the
words of Horace, *carpe diem.*

SIR JOHN SUCKLING[1]

A LYRICAL PIG POET[2]

Encouragements to a Pigling

*W*HY so wan and pale, fat pigling?
Prythee why so wan?
Didst thou dream thy parts were sizzling
In a frying pan?
Prythee why so wan?

Why so dumb and dull, fat pigling?
Prythee why so dumb?
Has the thought of *real pigskin* [3]
Made thee look so glum?
Prythee why so dumb?

Quit, quit, for shame! Back to thy trough!
Pigs all must perish.
Go stick thy snout into that scoff
Which all pigs cherish[4]
And munch with relish!

---

1. Sir John Suckling the Pig Poet, not to be confused with Sir John Suckling the poet.
2. 'Easy, natural Suckling' – a Pig Poet of improvisation who would not, or could not, take pains.
3. The skin of pigs, chiefly used to make saddles and wallets.
4. Probably Tottenham Pudding; see 'On First Looking in the Pigman's Storehouse', Squeaks, p.23.

COLONEL RICHARD LOVELOUSE

A DASHING PIG POET[1]

From His Pen

*B*REEZE blocks don't make a prison drear,
   Nor corrugated iron.
A pig who keeps his fodder near
Cares not what he might lie on.

If I have turnips in my pen
   And pigmeal in good measure
Only the angel pigs[2] in heav'n
Can hope to know such pleasure.

1. Lovelouse, a pig whose life was one dramatic turbulent career. He never stood still for an instant.

2. 'Angel pigs': the heavenly hogs.

7

WALT WHITPIG[1]

AN IRREGULAR PIG POET[2]

The Humans

I THINK I could turn and live with humans
  they are so clever and adaptable;
I stand and look at them sometimes half the day long.
They, when they sweat, peel off a sweater;
They do not mess about in the rain without a good hat;
They do not make me sick pushing their backsides into my
  snout;
Not one of them has the itch; not one needs to scratch himself
  on the lumpy tree;
Not one bites his neighbour nor sits on his little ones' heads;
Not one nips another's tail with his sharp teeth over the whole
  earth.[3]

1. Whitpig was a Hampshire, as was Henry Wadsworth Longfarrow q.v.
2. He seemed unable to find free expression for his emotions until he hit upon the curious, irregular, recitative measures of 'Leaves of Grass'.
3. Whitpig was not the only Pig Poet to express an admiration for mankind.

Cf., for example, this gobbet of Walter Savage Landrace on the pigman's daughter:

> Ah, What avails the cloven race!
> Ah, what the form porcine,
> When every virtue, every grace!
> Rose Aylmer, all are thine.

9

WILLIAM COWPAT[1]

A COMPANIONABLE POET[2]

Verses

supposed to be written by Oswald Old Spot,[3] during his
solitary confinement in a sty constructed in a corner of
woodland in Gloucestershire[4] where he was, for the most
part, expected to forage for his own sustenance.

I AM master of all I survey
My right there is none to dispute
From my sty all around to my fence
I am lord of the nut and the root.
O Solitude! where is the charm
Which porkers have spied in thy eye.
Better squashed in a factory farm
Than to reign in this dump of a sty.

---

1. Pronounced *kú-pat*.
2. 'Cowpat, like a charming companion on a day's rooting, grunts delightfully about anything.'
3. Oswald Old Spot of Gloucester, pig of pigs, a boar famed in piglore. Cf. 'Oswald Old Spot of Gloucester', Belley, p.21.
4. At or near the source of the River Thames.

Not so much as a mis'rable runt[5]
To bite when I'm feeling alone.
How I miss the sweet music of grunt,
I start at the sound of my own.
The children who pass with their dog
Are pig-ignorant to a degree.
They don't know a boar from a hog,[6]
Their dullness is shocking to me.

5. A 'runt': an unusually small, weak, or stunted pigling, good only for 'thump therapy'. Such pigs, the weakest of the litter, are sometimes called *Benjamins*. The allusion is to Benjamin, the youngest son of Jacob (Genesis xxxv. 18). Again, they may be called *Anthonies*, after Saint Anthony's pig. Saint Anthony having been originally a swineherd, and being, therefore, the patron saint of pigs.

6. The distinction that Cowpat puts here into Oswald's mouth is the important one, to Oswald, that a hog is a castrated boar. This, however, is hog's secondary meaning, its first meaning describing the genus, *sus scrofa*.

Ah! cauliflowers, wurzles & co.
Divinely disposed upon swine.
O, had I the wings of a crow,[7]
How soon I would make you all mine.
My sorrows I then would erase
In the mercy of lashings of scoff
And my Pigman[8] I'd fervently praise
If I once got my snout in that trough.

7. A pigidiom.
8. Here Cowpat once again reveals that commendable faith in mankind which shines like a beacon through all his work. One thinks of his memorable line:

> Men move in a mysterious way
> their wonders to perform.

WILLIAM BELLYACHE

A MYSTICAL PIG POET

The Sick Pig

O PIG thou art sick.
  Th'indigestable worm[1]
Thou hadst for thy tea
Has made thee squirm,

Has visited thee
With a mystical joy[2]
And his dark wormey blood[3]
Does thy life destroy.[4]

---

1. The worm in question is the bloodworm, not properly a worm at all, but the larva of the midge Chironomus, some 13 mm. long, and probably picked out of stagnant water.
2. 'Mystical joy': Bellyache believed, fantastically, that pigs of his own breed — short, thin and with the distinctive high pale forehead and, for a pig, large eyes — were directly descended from the Pigs of the Ark. That is to say, from the senior of those two breeds that Noe (or Noah) took with him into the Ark (Genesis vii). Cf. his memorable lines:

And did those trotters yonks ago
Trot up the gangplank to the Ark. & co.

Bellyache was thus persuaded that his own breed of pig must be the original 'unclean beast' of Leviticus xi. It was this morbid and self-accusing belief that nurtured his own death-wish: 'I glory in dying', he was often heard to grunt.

3. Cf. Wobblebottom:

She never gave a grunt,
But let concealment, like a worm
  in the blood,
Feed on her rosy jowls.

4. Pighyperbole: the pig in question would be in no danger and, in a couple of days, would be frisking about again.

ROBERT BUMS

AN EGALITARIAN PIG POET[1]

To a Mouse

on turning her up[2] (her mate the while fleeing in panic up
the Pig Poet's left nostril) in her nest with his snout.

*W*EE sleekit,[3] cow'rin, tim'rous Mousie
I'm sorry for thy wee bit housie!
Gi'e my condolence to thy spousie
Gin he come out.
It must be awfu' dark and lousie
Up in my snout.

But Mousie, never peak nor pine,
Reflect how oft in Life's Design,
The best laid schemes o' Mice and Swine
gang up the spout;[4]
An so wee friend, for auld lang syne,[5]
Forgi'e my snout.

1. 'A pig's a pig for a' that', and all that.
2. While rooting for puddock-stools.
3. 'sleekit': sleek.
4. 'The best laid schemes etc.': a line much quoted in the pigfields of Caledonia.
5. 'For auld lang syne': for (the sake of implicitly happier) times gone by. The Pig Poet has not forgot that the Mouse is an old acquaintance.

JAMES HOGG[1]

A DIFFUSE PIG POET[2]

Our Gilts[3] are no but Piglings Yet

Oᴜʀ gilts are no but piglings yet,
  They're lichtsome lovely piglings yet;
It scarce would do
To jump the queue[4]
And gobble up their middlings[5] yet;
But there's a braw time coming yet
When we may gang a roaming yet
And some I twig
will be in pig[6]
Before I've finished po'ming yet.[7]

---

1. James Hogg the Pig Poet, not to be confused with James Hogg the Ettrick Shepherd.
2. Lack of early intellectual discipline made Hogg diffuse.
3. 'Gilt': a young female pig.
4. A rather nasty *double entendre* here, I fear ('queue' deriving from the Latin *cauda*, the tail). Nor, I suspect, can the next line be taken for granted.
5. 'Middlings': the coarser part of ground wheat.

6. 'In pig': girt in, *enceinte*.
7. The Pig Poets (all, as yet, male) find composition neither quick nor easy. Of them it may truly be said: *Ars longa, vita brevis*. Even the best poetry-producing breed (the Middle White) can only be expected to produce as many poems in a lifetime as a sow produces litters, say five or six. Wobblebottom was exceptional.

15

They're neither proud nor saucy yet;
They're neither plump nor gaucy[8] yet;
A bunch of jinking,[9]
Bonny blinking,[10]
Hilty-skilty[11] piglings yet.
But O their wrigglings are mair sweet
Than windfalls or than sugar-beet;
An' right or wrang,
Ere it be lang,
I'll hae them fore[12] my breakfast yet.

8. 'Gaucy': plump and jolly. A tittle of tautology here?

9. 'Jinking': frolicking, turning, dodging! That sort of thing!

10. 'Blinking': glittering. Cf. Middle English blenken.

11. 'Hilty-Skilty': helter-skelter, holter-polter (German) , in great hurry and confusion. Cf. Wobblebottom:

And helter-skelter have I trotted to thee.

12. A case has been made for *for* for *fore*; *fore* far better expresses the intention of the Pig Poet.

WILLIAM GRUNTSWORTH

———

The Worms

I FELT put out, like half a worm
 Whose other half has just been ate;
When all at once I saw one squirm,
A lovely worm, the biggest yet;
His head was fat as a tomato[2]
I had the darling for a starter.

Then! Blow me down and strike me mad
If I did not see worms galore!
A Poet could not be but glad[3]
To see them squirm across the floor.
Ten thousand saw I at a blink;
I scoffed them quick as you can wink.

1. No one has ever surpassed him in the power of giving utterance to some of the most elementary sensations of Pig confronted by the eternal spectacle of nature.

2. Pronounced *tom-arter*.

3. Pigbathos. By far the weakest line in the poem.

SIR WALTER SCOFF

AN HISTORIC PIG POET [1]

Crushinbor [2]

O YOUNG Crushinbor is come out of his straw,
Frae Hogsfield to Pigdon [3], he is the best boar.
As big as a barn and as strong as an ox,
With trotters like tree-trunks and muscles like rocks,
For serving a sow or for winning a war,
There never was pig like the young Crushinbor.

He came like a tractor, he came all alone,
He stayed not for ditch, and he stopp'd not for stone,
But ere he arrived at the trough by the gate
The swill had been guzzled. The hero came late.
So lusty in service, so fierce in war,
There never was pig like the young Crushinbor.

1. Scoff will always be an historic
Pig Poet and, that being so, some few
people from time to time will look
on his verses and a few will be found
to praise him.
2. Gordon Crushinbor: a character

from Caledonian piglore.
3. 'Frae Hogsfield to Pigdon': i.e.
through all the wide Border.
(Hogsfield, properly Hogganfield, is
near Glasgow. Pigdon is three miles
WNW of Morpeth in Northumberland.)

He squealed like two tomcats, he sucked like a louse,[4]
He frighted the piglings, he worried the sows,
He grunted like thunder, he snorted like smoke,
The piggy eyes narrowed, the porcine heart broke,
And with pangs in the belly that grieved him full sore,
Was never pig sick[5] like the young Crushinbor.

4. To suck like a louse: a pigidiom *outré* here; it is normally used of in-efficient weaners.

5. Not even 'The Sick Pig' in Bellyache's eponymous pig poem.

LORD BACONBUM[1]

A PASSIONATE PIG POET[2]

So We'll Go No More a Nutting

So WE'LL go no more a nutting
So deep into the wood,
Though the snout's still good for rutting[3]
And the nuts be just as good.

For the fence outwits the pig
And the food lies in the trough
And what pigling wants to dig
When some Pigman brings the scoff?[4]

Though the snout was made for rutting
And the nuts lie on the ground,
Yet we'll go no more a nutting
While there's pigmeal to be found.

1. George Gordon Noel, 6th Lord Baconbum of Newstead Abbey and Rochdale.
2. Passionately fond of nuts etc.
3. 'Rutting': digging ruts in the ground or, perhaps, a corruption of rooting. In any case, nothing to do with the copulation of deer.
4. Another important tenet of pig (Baconian) philosophy : 'What pigling wants to dig when some Pigman brings the scoff.' Cf. Baconbum's 'Hours of Idleness'.

PERCY BYGGE BELLEY

A GLOOMY PIG POET[1]

Oswald Old Spot of Gloucester

I MET a hog from Gloucester[2] at the Show[3]
Who said: Two vast and legless troughs of stone
Stand near our pig pen. Nearby used to grow
An ancient apple. Apples bruised and brown,

Tasting of wrinkly skin and mistletoe[4]
Of Bitter Pit[5] and grubs of Codling Moths[6]
And Sawflies[7] plus some Wasps and Ear-wigs,
Our Pigman used to heap into those troughs;

Until last spring, this boar, who said to me
Just call me Oswald Old Spot,[8] *pig of pigs,*
Rested his giant hams against that tree.

---

1. One who had rooted beneath the Upas Tree.

2. Gloucester Old Spot: a very old breed. A white pig with black spots and drooping ears that hang right forward over the face.

3. The Oxford County Show. The informant was Thomas Jefferson Hogg.

4. *Viscum album*, a plant parasitic on apple and other fruit trees.

5. A complex disorder in apple trees.

6. A pale pink grub which feeds on the central core of apples, sometimes also of pears and plums.

7. The grub of the apple sawfly, *Allantus cinctus*, a creamy-white grub which feeds on the central core of apples.

8. *Oswald Old Spot*, famous in pig-lore; a good specimen of his breed, with a straight top-line and exceptionally well-developed hams.

Not a lot now remains, only a jagged lump.
Around, as far as porcine eye can see,[9]
The black pig-trammelled mud surrounds the stump.

9. One furlong (201.17 metres).

JOHN SQUEAKS

A ROMANTIC PIG POET[1]

On First Looking in the Pigman's Storehouse

MUCH have I guzzled at the Common Trough
And many goodly Tott'nham Puddings[2] seen.
In every corner of this Field I've been
And foraged lots of Roots and Nuts and stuff.

Much of this Shed I've heard that I thought guff
The one the Pigman holds as his demesne,
And never in a million years I ween
Did I expect to see such loads of scoff.

Then felt I like some Gruntsworth[3] of the fell,
When a few thousand Worms about him creep,
Or like stout Baconbum[4] who, so they tell,

Trots where the Beech-nuts form a monstrous Heap,
Munching with all his Gilts, some Hogs as well,
Silent within a Wood, in Nuts jowl-deep.

1. One whose name was writ in water.
2. Tottenham Pudding: a concentrated form of swill, first produced by a workmen's pig club in Tottenham. (Squeaks was farrowed in Finsbury.)
3. William Gruntsworth, the nature-watching, worm-loving Pig Poet.
4. George Gordon Noel, 6th Lord Baconbum of Newstead Abbey and Rochdale, the stout and passionate Pig Poet.

HENRY WADSWORTH LONGFARROW[1]

A SHALLOW PIG POET[1]

The Large Black Boar[3]

*U*NDER a spreading chestnut tree
   The Large Black scoffs his nuts.
The Boar a mighty pig is he
With thunder in his guts,[4]
And the muscles of his brawny flanks
Are big as coconuts.

His hair is crisp and black and short,
His face is somewhat knowin',
His snout is wet with porcine sweat,
He eats whatever's goin'
And looks the Pigman in the eye[5]
To see what he might throw in.

1. Longfarrow was a Hampshire, a breed imported from North America. Prick eared, with a white saddle on a black body. Thick-set, quick-growing and used for cross-breeding.
2. As a Pig Poet Longfarrow was extremely popular during his lifetime and although his work lacks the real depth of great pig poetry his verse is still read widely and with pleasure.

3. 'Large Black': the most important of the black pigs, it has large lop ears. A good grazing pig, the sows are very docile.
4. 'Thunder in his guts': pigidiom equivalent to lead in his pencil.
5. He 'looks the Pigman in the eye': this the acknowledged first sign of a healthy, vigorous and alert pig.

Week in, week out, from morn to night,
You can hear him grunt and go;
You can see him swing his heavy hams
With measured beat and slow;
You can tell he's hung like the village bell
If you glimpse him from below.

And piglings coming back from scoff
Look in at the old Large Black;
They love to see, beneath that tree,
Him make the conkers crack,
And the loins that brought them into being
and the straight and noble back.

Thanks, thanks to thee, most worthy sire
For the service thou hast done,
Thou flaming forge of all our lives
We hope thou hadst some fun,
And we hope thou shalt have plenty more.

So squeak they everyone.

WILLIAM BARNS

A RUSTIC PIG POET [1]

Piglings' Poke [2]

Iɴ Piglings' Poke the yoller thissles
Teäste ov how this worl' began, [3]
And there vor pigs to wet their whissles, [4]
Water's bubblen in the pan;
An in the trog there's Tott'nham pud
An' barley meal and fishes' blud, [5]
But, 'tis no joke, the mighty woak [6]
Does best for pigs down Piglings' Poke.

1. Barns lived plump (sic) in the middle of Thomas Hoggety's Wessex. Barns, like Hoggety, was a Wessex Saddleback, a black pig with a white stripe around its body and white front feet. (Unlike the Essex Saddleback which has all four feet white and a white tip to its tail.) From Barns emanates the bold and broad Doric grunt of Dorset.
2. Ordnance Survey 1:63,360, sheet 178 (Dorchester) Grid Reference 514216, i.e. south of Puddletown, west of Piddlehinton.
3. Cf. 'To taste like the first sunrise': pigidiom.
4. Pigs' whistles.
5. 'Fishes' blud': white fish meal made from whole white fish (non-oily) which are ground up, bones and all. A useful source of pig protein.
6. 'Woak': oak tree.

In Zummertime the woak so pirty[7]
He[8] shiädes uz vrom the zun so keen,
An' with his mossy moot[9] so girty[10]
He's the pleäce to scratch or lean;
But when his leaves turn goldney brown,
An' acorns all come tumblin' down
Then tis no joke, the mighty woak
Does best for pigs down Piglings' Poke.

7. 'Pirty': pretty.
8. For pigs, as for Frenchmen and Germans, trees are masculine in gender.
9. 'Moot': the trunk of a tree or other large immovable object. Derivation uncertain.

10. 'Girty': gritty (Cf. 'pirty'). Not great as in 'gurt big 'uns'. Barns' 'girty moot' is equivalent to William Porker Yeats' 'lumpy tree'. (cf. also Walt Whitpig, p8.)

THOMAS PUDD

A DELIGHTFUL PIG POET[1]

I Remember, I Remember

I REMEMBER, I remember,
  The sty where I was born,
And Mother's lovely row of teats
That caught the sun at dawn.
It's funny I should still recall
The sow who farrowed me
And how my favourite nipple was
Left column, number three.

I remember, I remember,
The creep[2] where I would crawl
to get away from Mother who
Kept sitting on us all.
How often do I wish that she
had looked behind instead
of burkeing[3] brother Anthony[4]
by sitting on his head.

1. 'Sweet and delightful in every
way were the pig and his poetry.'
2. A sty is often fitted with a 'creep'
where the piglings can escape from a
clumsy or aggressive sow.
3. To burke: to smother or to
suffocate.

4. 'Anthony': the runt of the litter.
5. Cf. Gruntsworth:

  Heaven lies about us in our infancy!
  Shades of the slaughter-house begin
    to close
  Upon the growing pig.

I remember, I remember
How once I saw my pa,
(I was his thousandth little pig!),
That's he said my Mama.
He scratched his hams against our gate
And though we never met,
I often think about those hams,
The gate is swinging yet.

I remember, I remember
The swill bins looming high.
I used to think their rattling lids
Were close against the sky:
It was a pigling's ignorance,
But now it makes me dismal,
To think how close I was to heav'n
When I was infin'tes'mal.[5]

ALFRED LORD TENDERTUM[1]

A POWERFUL PIG POET[2]

The Charge of the Pig Platoon[3]

*H*ALF an egg, half an egg,
Half an egg custard[4]
Swims in a bucket of swill
not a lot fusted.[5]
Forward the Pig Platoon!
Charge for the macaroon![6]
up for the scoff we trot
Keener than mustard.

Buckets to right of us,
Buckets to left of us,
Buckets in front of us,
Rattle and clatter;
Nobly we gorge and scoff
Lots from the common trough,

1. Alfred Tendertum, 1st Baron Tendertum.
2. We can accept his own valuation of his powers: 'I don't think that since Wobblebottom there has been such a masterly Pig Poet as I – to be sure!'
3. Based on an actual happening at Farringford Home Farm.
4. 'Half an egg custard': a culinary disaster of Mrs Aylmer, the pigman's wife.
5. To fust: to become musty or mouldy. Cf. Wobblebottom: *Hamlet, Pig of Denmark*, (iv.4.39).
6. 'The macaroon': a culinary disaster of Rose Aylmer, the pigman's daughter.

Still there is not enough,
Sadly we wobble off,
Wiser and fatter.[7]

When can our glory fade?
O the keen charge we made!
More so than mustard!
Honour the Pig Platoon!
  – I missed the macaroon
But got some custard.

7. Pigidiom: to rise from the trough a
wiser and a fatter pig.

JOHN BUMBUM

A DREAMING PIG POET[1]

Song[2]

*W*HO would big turnips see
Let him come hither.
Parsnips and broccoli
Mashed up together
With some potato peel
And quite a lot of meal,
To make a pigling feel
He'll be a porker.

1. 'And as I walked through the wilderness of this world, I lighted on a certain place where was a Pen, and I laid me down in that place to sleep: and, as I slept, I dreamed a dream, – *The Pigling's Progress.*'

2. From *The Pigling's Progress From This World to That Which is to Come.*
3. 'Porridge': pigmeal mixed with a little water to make a stiff paste.

Who would be fat and round
Let him eat porridge[3]
But if none may be found
Then let him forage.
He'll keep his snout down low
Find lots of roots & co.
Until he feels, you know,
Almost a porker.

Hogget[4] nor baconer[5]
Can stop his troughing.
He'll always get his share
When he is scoffing.
Then fancies, hence! avaunt!
He'll fear no hogget's grunt.
He'll push right to the front
To be a porker.

4. 'Hogget': a young hog, a two-year-old.   5. 'Baconer': a bacon pig.

THOMAS HOGGETY[1]

AN AWARE PIG POET[2]

Weathers

*T*HIS is the weather the piglings love,
 And so do I;
When the chestnuts shake in the heav'ns above,
And conkers fly:
And the little brown beech nuts lie around,
And the acorns hide in the mouldy ground,
And a pig can't scoff what a pig has found,
And the piglings rut through the leafy mound,
And so do I.

This is the weather the piglings hate,
And so do I;
When the beeches drip and the scoff comes late
And nothing's dry:

1. Hoggety was (like Barns, q.v.) a Wessex Saddleback.
2. There is not one of Hoggety's poems that fails to add some insight to our own imperfect awareness of nature.

And the raindrops splash like a drowning crow,[3]
And the fence gives a kick like an elephant's toe,[4]
And the turnips lose their purple glow,[5]
And the piglings home to their pig-sties go,
And so do I.

3. 'To splash like a drowning crow':
a very common pigidiom.
4. An electrified fence.

5. The all-fascinating 'purple glow' of
the turnip. Cf. Porker Yeats, p39.

GERARD PIGLEY HOGSKIN

AN EXPERIMENTAL PIG POET [1]

Pig Beauty

G LORY be to God for pigs & co.
For titbits: rose-pink nipples in a double row;
For bristles all in stipple upon pigs that doss;

Sweet squawking, squeaking sucklings; squeals of sow,
Rumble, grumble and gruff of hogs that grunt and grow
And all gilts, their glitter, glamour and gloss.

All pigs snuffling, snouts in the common trough
Whatever is toothsome, tasty (Watch it go!),
With swift, sure swallowings, snouts atoss
They gobble-gorge and guzzle up their scoff
Then toddle off.

1. Hogskin's brave experiments were
born of a life-long tension between
pig and poet.

ROBERT LOUIS SADDLEBACK[1]

Song[2]

*G*IVE to me the scoff I love,
 Let the worms squirm by me,
Give the jolly heaven above
And the meal-tub nigh me.
Bed in the bush with stars to see,
Snout laid out in the clover –
There's the life for a pig like me,
There's the life for ever.

Let the blow fall soon or late,[3]
Let what will surround me;
I won't mind the fence and gate
If my grub is down me.
Worm I ask not, louse nor grub,
Nor a hog to gnaw me;
All I ask, the heaven above
And the trough before me.

---

1. Robert Lewis Balfour Saddleback, a British Saddleback, farrowed in Scotland, a black pig, with lop ears and a white band over the shoulders and front legs.

2. Set to an air by Schweinbert.

3. 'Let the blow fall soon or late': another neat expression of pig (Baconian) philosophy. Cf. 'Pigs all must perish', Sir John Suckling, p6.

RUDYARD PIGLING[1]

AN INSPIRATIONAL PIG POET[2]

If

I F you can hog the trough when all about you
Are missing out and blaming it on you,
If you can use your stiffened upper snout[3] too,
And snuffle out some nuts and roots to chew,
If you can mate and not be tired by mating
And sire half the pigs along the Ouse,[4]
And bite the loved ones' tails while you are waiting,
And make a gilt feel guilt should she refuse,

If you can sleep and dream and think it jolly,
And eat and sleep and dream and feel no shame,
If you can meet with cabbage and broccoli
And treat those *Cruciferae*[5] just the same,
If you can scoff your swill in half a minute
While half the other pigs are in the hay,
Yours is the Pigfield, chum, and all that's in it,
And- which is more – you'll be a PIG, OK!?

1. A Large White, a white, long,
quality pig with upright ears. The
standard British breed.
2. Pig poetry is not confined to the
squealings of defeatism.
3. The 'stiff upper snout': for Pigling,
a symbol of the best porcine tradition,
namely, keeping your head down
and minding your own business.
4. 'The Ouse': a river flowing
through Pigling's beloved Sussex.
5. 'Cruciferae': an order of *Hypogeous
exogens* including the cabbage and all
its varieties.

WILLIAM PORKER YEATS[1]

AN IRISH PIG POET[2]

Pig Instinct

I WILL arise and go now, and find a lumpy tree,
And scratch and scrape my backside, until it's time for scoff;
Nine minutes there should do me, and, like as not, I'll be
There on my own at the evening trough.

And I shall have some peas there, for peas come dropping slow,
Dropping from the pigman's bucket to porkers where they squeal,
Green the crisp kohl-rabi, turnips a purple glow,
And bran tubs full of barley meal.

I will arise and go now, for always night or day,
I've got this kind of instinct, when scoff is to the fore.
When I stand in a corner, or lie down in the hay,
I feel it in my deep heart's core.

1. Author of 'The Trough of Broth'.   William Porker Yeats is an Irish poet
2. He owed much to Ireland; but it is   and to remember that he is a Pig Poet.
sometimes worthwhile to forget that

RALPH HOGSON[1]

A PROSELYTISING PIG POET[2]

Tom,[3] You Old Bacon Pig

*T*OM, you old bacon pig
  Will you not stay,
Sleep on my thing'majig,[4]
Chew at my hay?

All things I'll give you
Will you be my guest,
Turnips and cabbages,
Nuts of the best,
Carrots and cucumbers,
Pumpkins and pears.
I'll scratch your back & co.[5]
And bite your ears,
Oh, and the piglings will
tempt you to play,

1. Hogson was a Yorkshire, the standard British breed (also known as Large White.)
2. A voice grunting in the wilderness, Hogson held the strong opinion that pigs should not be condemned to be slaughtered in their prime merely that Mankind might enjoy bacon, ham, gammon, sausages, chops, pigs' trotters, pork pies, boars' heads and so on.
3. 'Tom': a popular name for a pig.

Cf. the celebrated Welsh (or Welch) – white, long, bacon-type pig with lop ears – Pig Poet, Dylan Pig-Thomas:

> And I am dumb to tell the porker, Tom,
> How in my sty goes the same crooked worm.

4. 'Thing'majig': here, an insulated floor space.
5. '& co': … if you scratch mine.

Tom you old rover,
Why hasten away?

Last week the copse corner,
Last night the plough.
Morning, you're deep in mud,
Slumped in the slough;[6]
Thence to the apple tree
 – Windfalls again –
Only a moment
Then up to the plain,
Ten minutes rooting 'til
You've had enough,
Then with the rest of us
Up to the trough.[7]

Tom, you old bacon pig,
Will you not stay,
Sleep on my thing'majig,[8]
Chew at my hay?

6. 'Slough', rhyming with cow: a miry place out of which it is difficult (but not for pigs) to get. Cf. Bumbum's 'Slough of Despond'.

7. The typical itinerary of a dashing pig. Cf. Colonel Richard Lovelouse.

8. 'Thing'majig': this time, a bed of roses.

JOHN MAIZEMEAL

A STORY-TELLING PIG POET[1]

Swine Fever[2]

I MUST down to the ditch again, to the lonely ditch and the sky,
And all I ask is a fat worm and a star to munch him by,
and the soft mud and the snail's blood and the fat fleas soaring,
And the wet roots and the old boots and the hedgehog's snoring.

I must down to the ditch again, to the vagrant pygsy[3] life,
To the slug's way and the bug's way with a smell like the
    Pigman's wife,[4]
And all I ask is a patch of grass and a clump of clover
And a long snore for a prize boar when the munch is over.

1. His ability to tell a story in verse is reminiscent of Geoffrey Porker, the seminal Pig Poet.
2. 'Swine Fever': a notifiable disease; the police must be informed at once.
3. 'Pygsy': i.e. pig-gipsy.
4. The Pig Poet associates the Pigman's wife with the smell of Farm Foods. (Cf. Pavlov on 'Conditioned Reflexes'.)

ALFRED NOISE[1]

A RHYTHMIC PIG POET[2]

Harry the Hog[3]

*T*HE wind was a model of mildness among the chestnut trees,
The conkers were falling gently, borne by the balmy breeze,
The field was as quiet as a hedgehog;[4] as yet there was no scoff,
And Harry the Hog came trotting –
Trotting – trotting –
Harry the Hog came trotting, up to the old tin trough.

He'd a nasty scar on his forehead, where mother had bitten his
    chin,[5]
A coat of the finest bristle, a beautiful black hog's skin,
He kept it as clean as a whistle, as hogs are wont to do,
And he stopped to nibble a thistle,
Stopped, as one might, for a thistle
Stopped in his tracks for a thistle
With a flower of steely blue.[6]

1. One of the troublesome Noises.
2. The heartbeat of the lives and loves of pigs runs through his pig poems like an endless seam.
3. A comic character famed in piglore.
4. 'Quiet as a hedgehog': a pigidiom. Hedgehogs are proverbially quiet because they usually present to pigs by curling up into a small prickly ball. At night they may snore. Cf. Maizemeal's 'Swine Fever', p 42.
5. One of the most difficult lines in Pig Poetry. One can only assume the sow aimed for the chin or jowl and missed.
6. *Echinops ritro*, the Globe Thistle.

Up to the pig-trough he trotted, and banged with his snout on
   the tin,
And he looked in the trough and saw nothing, not even an
   onion skin;
He whistled[7] and squinted sideways, and there at the gatepost
   he saw
Rose, the pigman's daughter,[8]
The pigman's little daughter,
Skipping along with a bucket,
A bucket in either paw.

He rose right up on the pig trough; he couldn't move fast
   enough,
And she emptied her pails with a hurry, his face was covered in
   scoff,
And the sweet cascade of pigswill came tumbling over his snout,

---

7. A pig's whistle. Cf. the inn sign.   8. Rose Aylmer.

As he guzzled it down in an instant,
Every last bit in an instant,
Toddled back home in an instant
And languidly laid himself out.

And still when the wind blows mildly, among the chestnut trees,
And the conkers are falling gently, borne on the balmy breeze,
And the field is as quiet as a hedgehog because there is no scoff,
Harry the Hog comes trotting –
Trotting – trotting –
Harry the hog comes trotting, up to the old tin trough.

ROBERT DITCHES[1]

A FAVOURITE PIG POET[2]

Trough Without Scoff

*T*ROUGH without scoff, as when the Pigman's daughter[3]
Tripped, with her buckets, down the wooden ladder,[4]
So let the imprisoned swill escape and splat[5]
Stinking[6] about her head as she lay flat.

1. Robert Rank Ditches, a Middle White, shorter and thicker than the Large White breed and with a snub nose (a *dished* face), rather like a Pekinese dog. It is one of the finest pork and poetry producing breeds.
2. Harry Hogge knows what he likes.
3. Rose, the pigman's daughter.
4. Descending from the garner floor of the barn.
5. 'splat': splatter.
6. A rare example of pigempathy. To the Pig Poet the swill would smell 'mair sweet than windfalls or than sugar-beet'. (Hogg).

Tailpiece

*H*ow lovely is the porcine form!
  How beautiful the sow!
So soft and pink and sleek and warm
With nipples in a row.   H.H.

INDEX OF AUTHORS

INDEX OF FIRST LINES